INNKEEPER

INNKEEPER

JOHN PIPER

PAINTINGS *by* GLENN HARRINGTON

::: CROSSWAY

WHEATON, ILLINOIS

The Innkeeper

Copyright ©1998, 2011 by Desiring God Foundation

Published by Crossway
    1300 Crescent Street
    Wheaton, Illinois 60187

Cover Design: Studio Gearbox

Paintings by: Glenn Harrington

First printing 1998

Reprinted with new cover and new art 2011

Printed in the United States of America

ISBN: 978-1-4335-3025-8

PDF ISBN: 978-1-4335-3026-5

Mobipocket ISBN: 978-1-4335-3027-2

ePub ISBN: 978-1-4335-3028-9

Library of Congress Cataloging-in-Publication Data
Piper, John 1946–
 The Innkeeper / John Piper.
  p. cm.
 ISBN 13: 978-1-58134-027-3 (alk. paper)
 ISBN 10: 1-58134-027-3
 1. Jesus Christ—Nativity—Poetry. 2. Hotelkeepers—Bethlehem—
Poetry. 3. Christian poetry, American. I. Title.
PS3566.I5915   1998
811'.54—dc21   98-36322

Crossway is a publishing ministry of Good News Publishers.

LB 21 20 19 18 17 16 15 14 13 12 11
14 13 12 11 10 9 8 7 6 5 4 3 2 1

TO ROLLIN

And All Who Ever Lost

A Child

A WORD *from* JOHN PIPER

So quickly do we pass over the Christmas words, "Herod . . . slew all the male children . . . two years old and under." But the poet lingers, weeping, raging, looking at the dark spot, in hope that any prick of light might become a portal for the sun. And what he sees he strains with words to show—pressing us against the perforation in the wall of pain.

Why this struggle? Why does the poet bind his heart with such a severe discipline of form? Why strain to give shape to suffering? Because Reality has contours. God is who He is, not what we wish or try to make Him be. His Son, Jesus Christ, is the great granite Fact. His hard sacrifice makes it evident that our spontaneity needs Calvary-like discipline. Perhaps the innkeeper paid dearly for housing the Son of God. Should it not be costly to penetrate and portray this pain?

The Innkeeper seeks to reveal the Light that shines behind this brutal moment in history and our own path of suffering.

Come and see!

Jake's wife would have been fifty-eight
The day that Jesus passed the gate
Of Bethlehem, and slowly walked
Toward Jacob's Inn. The people talked
With friends, and children played along
The paths, and Jesus hummed a song,
And smiled at every child he saw.

*H*e paused with one small lass to draw
A camel in the dirt, then said,
"What's this?" The girl bent down her head
To study what the Lord had made.
She smiled, "A camel, sir!" and laid
Her finger on the bulging back
Where merchants bind their leather pack.
"It's got a hump." "Indeed it does,
And who do you believe it was
Who made this camel with his hump?"
Without a thought that this would stump
The rabbi guild and be reviled,
She said, "God did." And Jesus smiled.
"Good eyes, my child. And would that all
Jerusalem within that wall
Of yonder stone could see the signs
Of peace!" He left the lass with lines
Of simple wonder in her face
And slowly went to find the place
Where he was born.

*F*olks said the inn
Had never been a place for sin,
For Jacob was a holy man.
And he and Rachel had a plan
To marry, have a child or two,
And serve the folks who traveled through,
Especially the poor who brought
Their meal and turtledoves, and sought
A place to stay near Zion's gate.

They'd rise up early, stay up late,
To help the pilgrims go and come,
And when the place was full, to some,
Especially the poorest, they would say,
"We're sorry there's no room, but stay
Now, if you like, out back. There's lots
Of hay, and we have extra cots
That you can use. There'll be no charge.
The stable isn't very large,
But Noah keeps it safe." He was
A wedding gift to Jake because
The shepherds knew he loved the dog.
"There's nothing in the Decalogue,"
He used to joke, "that says a man
Can't love a dog!"

*T*he children ran
Ahead of Jesus as he strode
Toward Jacob's inn. The stony road
That led up to the inn was deep
With centuries of wear, and steep
At one point just before the door.
The Lord knocked once, then twice, before
He heard an old man's voice, "'Round back!"
It called. So Jesus took the track
That led around the inn.

The old
Man leaned back in his chair and told
The dog to never mind. "Ain't had
No one to tend the door, my lad,
For thirty years. I'm sorry for
The inconvenience to your sore
Feet. The road to Jerusalem
Is hard, ain't it? Don't mind old Shem.
He's harmless like his dad. Won't bite
A Roman soldier in the night.
Sit down." And Jacob waved the stump
Of his right arm. "We're in a slump
Right now. Got lots of time to think
And talk. Come sit and have a drink.
From Jacob's well!" he laughed. "You own
The inn?" the Lord inquired. "On loan,
You'd better say. God owns the inn."

At that the Lord knew they were kin,
And ventured on: "Do you recall
The tax when Caesar said to all
The world that each must be enrolled?"
Old Jacob winced, "Are north winds cold?
Are deserts dry? Do fishes swim
And ravens fly? I do. A grim
And awful year it was for me
When God ordained that strange decree.
How could I such a time forget?

"Why do you ask?" "I have a debt
To pay, and I must see how much.
Why do you say that it was such
A grim and awful year?" He raised
The stump of his right arm. "So dazed,
Young man, I didn't know I'd lost
My arm. Do you know what it cost
For me to house the Son of God?"
The old man took his cedar rod
And swept it 'round the place: "Empty.
For thirty years alone, you see?

Old Jacob, poor old Jacob, runs
It with one arm, a dog . . . no sons.
But I had sons . . . once. Joseph was
My firstborn. He was small because
His mother was so sick. When he
Turned three, the Lord was good to me
And Rachel, and our baby Ben
Was born, the very fortnight when
The blessed family arrived.

And Rachel's gracious heart contrived
A way for them to stay–there in
That very stall. The man was thin
And tired. You look a lot like him."
But Jesus said, "Why was it grim?"
"We got a reputation here
That night. Nothing at all to fear
In that we thought. It was of God.

*B*ut in one year the slaughter squad
From Herod came. And where do you
Suppose they started? Not a clue!
We didn't have a clue what they
Had come to do. No time to pray,
No time to run, no time to get
Poor Joseph off the street and let
Him say good-bye to Ben or me
Or Rachel. Only time to see

A lifted spear smash through his spine
And chest. He stumbled to the sign
That welcomed strangers to the place,
And looked with panic at my face,
As if to ask what he had done.
Young man, you ever lost a son?"
The tears streamed down the Savior's cheek.

H e shook his head, but couldn't speak.
"Before I found the breath to scream
I heard the words, a horrid dream:
'Kill every child who's two or less.
Spare not for aught, nor make excess.
Let this one be the oldest here,
And if you count your own life dear,
Let none escape.' I had no sword,
No weapons in my house, but Lord,

I had my hands, and I would save
The son of my right hand. . . . So brave,
O Rachel was so brave! Her hands
Were like a thousand iron bands
Around the boy. She wouldn't let
Him go, and so her own back met
With every thrust and blow. I lost
My arm, my wife, my sons—the cost
For housing the Messiah here.

Why would he simply disappear
And never come to help?" They sat
In silence. Jacob wondered at
The stranger's tears.

I am the boy
That Herod wanted to destroy.
You gave my parents room to give
Me life, and then God let me live,
And took your wife. Ask me not why
The one should live, another die.
God's ways are high, and you will know
In time. But I have come to show
You what the Lord prepared the night
you made a place for heaven's Light.
In two weeks they will crucify
My flesh. But mark this, Jacob, I
Will rise in three days from the dead,
And place my foot upon the head
Of him who has the power of death,

And I will raise with life and breath
Your wife and Ben and Joseph too,
And give them, Jacob, back to you
With everything the world can store,
And you will reign forever more."